The Breath that Lightens the Body

The Breath that Lightens the Body

poems by

Deirdre Dwyer

Porcepic Books
an imprint of

Beach Holme Publishing
Vancouver

This book is published by Beach Holme Publishing, #226—2040 West 12th Ave., Vancouver, BC, V6J 2G2. This is a Porcepic Book.

We acknowledge the generous assistance of The Canada Council and the BC Ministry of Small Business, Tourism and Culture.

THE CANADA COUNCIL | LE CONSEIL DES ARTS
FOR THE ARTS | DU CANADA
SINCE 1957 | DEPUIS 1957

Editor: Joy Gugeler
Production and Design: Teresa Bubela

Cover Image: *Majcha*, a half-human, half fish creature, one of two kinds of mermaids in Thai culture. Artist: Attasart Tularak.

Canadian Cataloguing in Publication Data

Dwyer, Deirdre.
  The breath that lightens the body

Poems.
(A Porcépic Book)

ISBN: 978-0-88878-394-3

I. Title.
PS8557.W93B73 1999   C811'.54   C99-910307-5
PR9199.3.D92B73 1999

For Hans

Contents

For thousands of years the Chinese have sought to channel, harness and harmonize environmental forces, such as wind and water, to improve the landscape and, ultimately, their lives.

The re-creation of nature's patterns when siting a building or arranging its rooms and furniture will imbue the occupants with positive and balanced energy, and that energy will propel them along a fruitful and fortuitous life course. If, on the other hand, occupants are poorly placed—vis-à-vis the natural rhythms of the universe—their lives will be out of step, unbalanced, and a constant struggle.

— Sarah Rossbach, *Interior Design with Feng Shui*

JAPAN

I would like to step out
And be on the other side, and be a part of all

That surrounds me. I would like to be
In that solitude of soundless things, in the random
Company of the wind, to be weightless, nameless.

— Mark Strand, *Dark Harbor*

Sayonara letter
(for my nephew)

Halifax. Five a.m. Sandalwood on the table where the
sayonara gifts are still in wrapping. What can I tell
you about Tokyo's crowded streets, its hours a day
ahead; about geishas and kimonos; about sushi, sashimi—
food I have yet to taste? I see your sleepy five-year
old face trying to harden itself against goodbye. Children
are the first to learn how we do this. Leaving is a gift I
have yet to open.

My nerves walk linear paths and then they jump in
electrical dances. But only now can I rehearse our
talk after a bedtime story—I will tell you my leavings,
show you picture books and the globe—Tokyo only a
dot. Will you enclose all your schoolwork in letters?
Then I might feel I have traces of everyone—changes
in you and your sisters, the compression of everyone's life.

I'm suddenly crying, my nerves minnows at the water's
edge. I'm beginning to think you have a net and I
might let you pull me along. Everyone else doing the
same but you are more agile, you find me, pull me and
let me go again. I will return in the shape of a carp
and we will swim.

Spring's temple

Go past the overturned umbrellas
that hang from railings
catching the first minutes of spring,
past the orchard blossoms
of burgundy and peach bonsai
trees at your feet.
Look once and then go past
this—the suburb of spring.

A boy of ten, with many questions
will circle you. What can you say
but   *gomen nasai   wakarimasen*
shrugging your shoulders?
A temple roof beckons
like Fuji-san whispering to the clouds.
A pipe under a tiled slope
drips
into an open well.

In the air musky incense.
I read the beautiful scratchings
on a sign shaped like a house-on-stilts,
its mysterious code: trails of ink
shaping themselves as they flow,
the rose bush losing its petals.
Waxy green leaves,
petals of tea rose
settle in the earth-dry shadows.

Even a stone in the alders
—monument or tombstone?—
its fading whispers, vertical
paths delicate,
and carved.

Lessons of Sugamo

English is neither a revelation nor a thirst.
It's a spin of the globe
      —green, yellow, pink countries
becoming one colour, a planet
at the far end of a system.

Golden Week, after the school year's begun,
we settle in to "What are your hobbies?"

      "I play ski" and "I sleep."

But sleep is not a hobby, I tell them,
until they teach me the pattern
of school trips, Saturday classes,
rules and exams.

Street noises: motorcycles revving up,
trains rumbling in to the station, school girls rush
to first class, nodding quickly
at their *sensei*. The word implies wisdom,
respect, discipline,
the tip of a brush.

The clap of wooden *geta*,
an old woman steps by in grey kimono.
Can I take your picture? I gesture
as patiently, silently she answers,
knowing I cannot steal her soul.

Hirohito's birthday

Emperor—
                reminds me
of nursery rhymes, pandas,
                far away countries,
the curse and blessing of seclusion
like Rapunzel with her long hair.

We enter the palace courtyard,
the air hushed with planned restlessness.

Then everyone waves paper flags
while high above us behind glass
the Emperor is waving
—86 years old today—
his humble   arigato.

Thousands of round red suns.
I continue on through Imperial Gardens,
finding in a grove of trees
insects and spiders,
a secret mythic world
the crows must share
and they are bragging.

Iris Festival

Late June
huge islands of irises
beyond the park gate
where *obasan*
is singing folk songs.

For every song
there are a hundred flowers.

But not flowers, enigmas
of hand-made paper,
falling stars,
tails of meteors and comets,
elegies.

The red iris
is velvet *ikebana*.
The white iris
with blood veins
was once *obasan*.

Fishermen at Mizumoto Park

They have all the quietude
of Renoir's Sunday afternoons.
This river, Mizumoto—
                    original water,
green and placid
with its only fish
dying slowly
in this wet
lethargy.

The fishermen—
their straw umbrella hats,
their dry feet falling out
of sandals,
their fishing poles hanging
like question marks
cast out, in exile.

Rowboats paralyzed
in the middle of the river,
fishermen perched in them
like little buddhas.
Close to the bank
abandoned boats
drowning in algae.

No one's employed to push

1

Dark space, dark river,
a sullen underworld
at the bottom of night—beneath escalators
and stone steps the crowd reels,
waiting to be carried away from sake,
the neon lights of Shinjuku.

From behind thick pillars
the repetition and rounds,
amazing words:

> mamonaku nibansen ni
> densha ga maerimasu
> abunai desu kara...

Something dangerous.
Kanji on the white tiled wall
on the other side of the track—the dash
that ends each brushstroke.

2

In daylight the trains
on rails above the city
are matchbox toys.
At night the windows glow,
paper lanterns
we may never see again.

The train lurches
and coughs into the rush hour.
Wrists and elbows
moan and creak
as the crowd presses in.

It is *hito-gomi* :
                    people - trash.

Night can be as bad
or worse—red eyes, roaming hands,
inebriated English.

Safer to stay at home
and wait for earthquakes.

Tokyo Light

Oh, cities and the light that never fails!

Late afternoon,
the silhouette of buildings,
the sun dusts the sky
with a powder you can't find
in women's boutiques.

The dusted sky reminds me
of all the cities of the world
at this hour: Montmartre
and old buildings leaning slightly
in their orbit, the radius
of Paris light and joie de vivre.

Pubs in London, the warm beer, and streetlights,
the Tower of London crows
in the afternoon.

There are artists here:
Turner in Tokyo Bay—
            burning ships and burning light?
Gaugin painting the azaleas in Komagome?
the kimonos?   Women in them,
their own gentle islands.

The light fails
only if we're not moved by it,
if we ignore what it's doing,
a simple delicate thing like breathing,
writing your name,
or throwing open a fan.

Singing Tatami

She's hiding in the bamboo wood.
Her *obi* sash
green Meiji brocade,
her dainty footfalls
and whisperings of a world
where you pillow
for the moment of Cloud and Rain.

O Tatami-san—not tall,
her breasts small and promising.
She sits overlooking the garden,
sits on her feet—
despises shoes.

Her cleanliness
is more than etiquette,
is her very fibre and strand.
Clouds weep by
and the sun, for a moment
lifts her breast.

In the poise of nipple and light
she yawns, stretches languid,
loses herself in a folk song / *enka*,
becomes a field of rush
before it is cut down
to cover thick straw mats, Japanese flooring
which takes her name,
her brocade,
her life.

Still Life

A long diamond
of sun on a silver kettle
stretches on the wall,
slips like a cup
into a saucer
into a bucket on the floor.

Watching this, a Japanese Venus
rises out of a cloud of steam,
like one of Yoshitoshi's geisha
bored as she leans over
the railing of a pleasure boat.

The scroll of the body

The sunlight thinks arms and legs
are sturdy stalks of bamboo,

                twice hyphenated.
I lounge in *sunlight shiatsu*:
Behind an ankle a camellia
bursts into canals,
the crests of the rivers' waves.
Fingertips, the bottom of feet—
how pink they are waiting
to touch.

Veins: a violet and sea-green web
or a branch, the rain
that you can't hear falling.

And hands, feet a careful arrangement
of bones, threads of ink calligraphy

—as if there's a secret book
with transparent pages, overlapping
maps of the body
like an antique scroll,
a city with underground passages,
winding tunnels
that write old syllabaries.

Tea Ceremony

In the *sensei's* home and gallery:
flowers in a pyramid of stone,
calligraphy on the wall
and painted fans from every era.

In a special alcove, *tokonoma*
a handwoven scroll of delicate
braided pastels bordering
the careful brush
of pen *shodo*.

A woman in silver kimono
serves chrysanthemum *sake*—
three yellow petals in a clear rice wine.
When she turns to leave autumn on her *obi* sash
is gold, silver and rust.

The ceremony begins: legs folded under
to sit on tatami and watch
as *sensei* scoops out
the green green powder, *matcha*,
dips a thin wooden ladle
into a kettle, filling the bowl,
and bamboo whisks the tea into a froth
of green: spirit of zen, ballet of wrist.

You cannot pivot
on ignorance—clockwise three rotations
and then you drink, wiping clean the bowl

before others drink
and it is cleansed, returned
and re-turned again:
essence of orbit,
clouds over the moon.

Tsukuba Planetarium

We enter the dome of stars,
Haruka, Chiharu and I,
leave evening outside
like a goddess under the trees.
Inside night falls early.
Cassiopeia chases Aquarius
or Mozart as flute and harp concertos
leave traces, vapour trails,
somersaults and figure eights.

Haruka's name means   far away.
A five year old
asleep now on her mother's lap.

This morning she brought me a kitten,
its eyes not yet open,
her wordless welcome,
gesture of initiation.

Around Haruka there are musical notes,
invisible kimono,
               Fuji-san mist
which may lift,
to reveal the peak
of that distant mountain.

The thin walls

"We are quiet lovers" he says.
You have to be in this country.

A print of a Japanese woman,
her kimono scattered around her,
one breast revealed
hangs on the wall of a distant gallery.
She is holding a book in her mouth.
Somewhere outside the frame
a man is coming inside her
but she can't make a sound.

The only sound of love
is the book falling.
The book opens, pages turn.
He dresses.

"We are quiet lovers, good lovers" he says.
When we make love
the sound of my breathing and his,
the small sounds of my body talking,
saying "yes" "yes" "this way" "here,"
words of a closed book.

Apprentice geisha

The loose edges make you feel irrepressibly
untamed. The secret that's yours
blatant on your skin.
Hands through your hair
gelled with instant coffee,
the white chocolate of love,
the pale wet pancakes.

You are wild
and headstrong from lack of sleep;
all the stained blankets in a heap
at the foot of the bed.

Everything is potent:
winter sun wanting
to harden your face to stone.

> Oh, the folds of your long black skirt,
> a purple sweater wrapped
> around his nakedness,
> the hair on his chest.

At the end of the day the crowded train as wild
as faculties that temporarily unleashed you.
Early moonlight on the Sumida river.
The edges of the day hemmed.
Everything rampant
tucks itself in.

Paper, scissors, stone

The strange euphoria
of sleeping with you,
persimmons bursting orange
on the trees behind stone walls.
The path we take to your house
as you wheel your bicycle
through the midnight streets.

On your wall posters of old Kyoto's roofs
terraced with snow,
a pale map of Canada
eclipsed by a vibrant red sun.

So as I wait for you now
I think about the shallow things we have
that we could lose
and *jankenpon,* the children's game
that decides who will be "It."

Outside an open window
a red bird perches on the limb of a tree.
Far below, a brook
banks a clean slope
of chalk, brick, rock.

Struck by *inabikari*
(for Steve & Valerie)

Lightning:
bracelets of pink silver,
random tremors,
tambourines tossed in the sky.

Nothing out here
at the edge of this world
feels the summer night's
wet heat. No one but
the snake that tunnels
through the weeds and tall grass
along the river bank.

Everyone seasons away
as I watch Japanese children light sparklers,
hold them out their livingroom windows

as I stand on your fifth floor balcony
caught in a world made lonely
by an act of nature,
lightning from cloud to cloud
that will not touch me.

Shinkansen to Akita

Train windows a country long.

Birds swoop low over the land.
Brooks fall into rivers.

The strange beauty—
of three crows flying in formation
above rice fields,
                        the challenge of
the huge leaves of a lotus
like kites rooted in water.

Akita Rain

Rain falls into a pond. Fat drops
between lotus leaves,
kites pulled down
into the murky green mud.
Like a lotus bud, the turn
of magazine pages that curl
around a moistened thumb.

Half an hour away
is yesterday's beach.
The sound of rain now
on its Japanese thatched roof
and the stunted trees,
on Sapporo cans in the sand
and the gravelled lane
that leads to empty cabins.
In beach-side gardens foxglove
and wilted hydrangea whisper
    gomen nasai   gomen nasai / I'm sorry.

               The sun is speechless
but the rain speaks both English
and Japanese, talks me into
ten bright pages
as it shakes the sand
from my ears.

Fireworks

Windows opening to weeds,
bonsai garden, long green fields.
Hanging open on a clothesline,
                              a summer *yukata*
a petticoat scarecrow,
its dry cotton charismata.

And the older flash of *o-hanabi*
lighting the sky before we arrive. We talk
as we pass traffic and walk
hayai, our language not broken
but braided.

Stumbling, we crawl down the slope
toward the river,
setting our blanket out. The moon
orange above
                    the flower-light.

Time to leave

Pink blooms of lotus by the bus depot
and paper Kanto lanterns ten metres high—
feats of balancing, prayers for the harvest
yet to come.

        I think myself back to the beach:
to young girls in bathing suits with skirts,
who run up to me
                and stare.

The tide high, a yacht parked
behind Hiroshige's wave.
Gulls circle low.
Eel grass, swords bent in the sand.

On the main road, I glance back
at the sun behind a cloud.
The last swimmers float
among the waves.

Climbing a mountain to the north

I dream 17th century men
like Basho making his pilgrimage
along the green highways of the Central Mountain.
How from the tops of mountains they discovered
misty towns in the distance below.
How it was all promise
clouded with fatigue.

Then I come upon a shrine,
its procession of monks ceremonial,
single-file and solemn on the path.
They costume the mountain,
these men whose reverence
and loyalty is to an ancient time
and cloaked in a curious bright silk.

Beach-combing, Rebun Island

On the northern Flower Island,
300 species of alpine plants,
winding roads, green hills
above coastal towns
and rugged rock.

Last night on the ferry Otaru's lights,
glass beads falling to the floor,
beer and *edamame*
with the Japanese
who chortled as drink rouged
their inexplicable faces.

Cans of sweet coffee this morning
in Rishiri's port town

before Rebun:
a piece of cliff is an arrow
between the sea and hills
that fall in
                and out of

what I came for.

Tanabata

Momoiwa surrounded by the quiet hills
of Rebun sets its own time
for this Christmas in August,
this festival of the stars:
all the magpies in the world
form a winged bridge so the lovers, Vega
and Altair, can cross the Milky Way
once a year to meet.

Donuts, popcorn, *udon* for sale,
and coloured paper *tanzaku* wishes
folded around bamboo.
                              Songs too,
a Japanese guitarist
on the roof
                    shouting the words.

And one foreigner at the festival
trying to sing along.

Leaving Rebun

Hold a tape recorder to the island's heart.
What will you hear
                            but friends
familiar and anonymous waving, clapping,
singing from the dock as the boat pulls out.
Commotion later, heads turning to find
two and then three dolphins
cavorting in the ferry's wake.

The northern fields of Wakkanai:

afternoon meadows
yellow in the distance,
brown-eyed susans
like grounded constellations.
Their shyness blushes, glistens.

And Queen Anne's lacy umbrellas,
pink around their edges.

What susan do the dark eyes name?

I wonder
if strawberries
are ripe at home?

Lonely Planet

Shiretoko is Ainu for end of the Earth.
Place of waterfall,
of the Cape fogged in,
of hot spring, sightings of deer
—*shika*
and fox—*kitsune*

of dreary souvenirs.

Sapporo's Botanical Garden

The slim volume of verse
in her pocket today is superfluous,
this day of dreams and lyrics, of time lost.

Clouds turn back, then are blown askew,
become fish bone,
nervous sparrows
a white horse
                    like Pegasus
is born from them,
playfully kicking her hooves into the blue.

Above her, a child's dragon
attempts ferocity. From its mouth nothing
but fanciful monsters above the treetops.

Through paths, women and children
meander, wander
defenceless, pass out of sight
behind tree trunks,
re-appearing as if the trees
have brought forth life.

These luminous summer apparitions:
girls in white dresses,
boys in white shorts,
the shadow of leaf,
pine needles hiding faces.
I try to walk away.
Reverie generous as rhyme.

A Japanese Christmas

In April, the cherry blossoms
litter the sidewalk
like the aftermath of a wedding.

The winding streets of Nakadai
a network of voluptuous leaves
and flowers—pink and maraschino red
azaleas and the blue tongues of irises
wilting or wilted
aching to speak.

I've been waiting for my sister's
promised gifts—
tonight has blossomed
brown paper!   My name
in black marker.
I unfold
red and green foil,
watery red ribbons, letters:
one for each of the months
since New Year's.
And more: a drawing of a happy face
sun, and   *What did you get for Eater?*

Earrings too like ragged moons,
and photos, their absolute eyes,
the small bodies of her children.
I long to know these strangers
with a Christmas-heavy heart in an April
so many years away from
that one day of giving.

April 25, 1989
Nakadai, Tokyo

Letter to Elissa

Sometimes I think I travel
only to come home
to my letterbox full of words from friends.
More than full, it surpassed
my expectations. I travel
the great country of susceptibility.

And your letters—

                          beautiful
summer-long descriptions of social news
and weather—an archaeological scroll
complete with middle names.

I thrive on words. They are my health,
the muscle I need
to transport me.

Words to net the land and pull
this country into a new theory
of continental drift.

Rotenburo in the snow

I am a lady of the lake in the woods,
hot spring, *onsen*, pond of rising mist.
The waters open for snowflakes
like early blossoms of plum or cherry,
like the sky raining *sake*.

Rotenburo in the morning alone
with snow and warm water,
I'm an Arthurian priestess,
an apprentice living a Japanese
screen-printed dream.

Surrounded by lamps
in the gentle forested hills,
by quiet trees, the leaves
of last autumn,
the sculpture of rock
and stone steps
down to the mist,
I am cleansed.

You cannot say *kekko* /enough
until you've seen Nikko
or neighbouring Nasu.
Now I have taken
more than sufficient
warm water.

HONG KONG

"But we shall drink 'wine of snakes', and perhaps..."
"Wine of snakes?"
"You know we have various magic wines—of snakes, of monkeys, of chickens. We pour blood of these animals in the barrels and the wine acquires magic power. He who drinks wine of snakes gets courage and strange curiosities. You will see."

— Nikos Kazantzakis in China

Letter from Hong Kong

A city with no easy answers,
a swamp of loud sentences that never stop,
rumours I wake to reluctantly.

The Chinese perform t'ai chi at dawn
despite roosters crowing, dogs barking.
Uneven landscape:
fitful hills pour into shantytowns.
In Wah Fu men carry birds around in their cages.
And Michael's blackbirds squawk
banter, retorts, rebuttals.

The language of the downtown
like its skyline of loose vowels, graffiti,
and Victoria Peak estates:
old dragons perched on the hillside
hide behind shrubs, tall gates
as I look down on the overcast city,
at the harbour's boats strung out
like souvenir shops along the Golden Mile.

I am Cinderella in sampan floating
through a slum of houseboats.
Behind me the backdrop of high-rises
at the foot of the mountain, the floating Jumbo restaurant
with its garish gold trim, its pervasive baroque.

To be the boy, his apron grey with fish stains,
who's throwing a pail of brown water
into the bay...

The day I leave
one of Michael's blackbirds is loose
on the balcony, shrieking,
opening its wings.

Preparation

Late afternoon,
at a long window a woman
looks down at Kowloon,
planning how best to
get to the island tomorrow,
sullen questions and strategies
huddled around her
like tourists around the bins
in Stanley's open-air market.

She will be here when I've gone.

This time next week
Phillipino women and girls
will again gather in squares downtown,
picnicking, busily chatting
on this, their one day off.
They will be oblivious to
Sunday's sombre character
and the woman who shoulders
its liabilities.

She will be the ghost, for me,
of the 11th floor, one of the
unforgettable, nameless,
a silhouette of ambivalence.

THAILAND

Be thou the lotus, let me be the bee,
To court and suck and make much of thy pollen.
Be thou the water, let me dragon be
That I praise and enjoy, once in thee fallen.

> — Sunthon Phu, from "Lines written near
> the statue of the Buddha of Prathom"

A secret about a secret: the more it tells you, the less you know.

> — Diane Arbus

Bo Phut

1
Linen white sky,
driftwood on the beach, Bo Phut,
coconut palms in an afternoon squall,
the serrated, long fringe of their arms.

Have you ever been here?

I write letters to friends wanting to get it right,
everything,
            all of it on paper:
the international chatter
of French children, Germans, Swedish girls.

I come away with sounds, textures,
small bowls of hot sauce,
spicy Thai seafood and curry.

Have you heard about the boy who drinks tabasco?

2
Foreign countries have no mirrors.

How to get it right: the sense
of looking, not looking, living all day
a still life of naked limbs.

3
Have you ever been to where the beach curves?

I have been to that country
where we travel each minute,
a fiction of luxury and fact.
I come away with a body
I do not know.

Samui

This rock is a seabird
sleeping forever deep within
its markings, its camouflage of feathers.

The locket of knit and purl and knot
of seaweed is a net
cast by water gods
         or reclusive peasants,
a parchment of ebb tide.

I hike my sundress up
around me, baring my legs.

I court a thousand eyes:
the passive, shy, wearied eyes
of fishermen and wives and frail children.

When I turn my back
my audience will climb out
of hiding

                wondering what
I will do next; I am not distrusted,
only a curiosity, a woman
walking away from precedent.

Dear Agatha

A perfect cast,
an island, high tensions in the constant sun.
Bo Phut beach, Smile Resort:

                    palm trees

and angry voices.
             "I will kill you " he said.

He is German or Swiss, recuperating from some illness;
she Thai with a foreign passport.
They quarrel over money, other lovers.
He shouts at her family, too.
What to make of this?

The English couple with a child,
a daughter. The mother once worked
in a Spanish circus—a dubious past.

An elderly army man, talking
unaware the war is over.
They drown in mystery.

What will become of it,
this murder, this body to be found
floating face down in the pool?

Early Dusk: A Theory

Rays of sunlight tight as wires
attached to your skin.

The day in the courtyard
is over; the wires
are pulled,
        cut.

All day I hardly speak;
language fails in the sun,
images evaporate...except for

        a Thai woman walking,
      pushing her sun-umbrella up,
      stepping down upon white gravel.

Thais rent the sun to travellers,
name their properties Calm,
Oasis, Peace, Paradise.

Early dusk,
people recede to their bungalows
—hour of reinstatement,
we drift to verandah chairs,
to a few pages of a book.

Now Thai children swim,
their faces talcum-powdered
all day under the shade of palms.

Green Stories

I want to tell you about the palm trees
                            —long green feathers

that remind me of
a small faded red atlas,
a poem my father transcribed.

              Oh, East is East
              and....

The palms are earrings for elephants,
lovers for the octopus, sacred cousin
to the sea anenome.

They draw water from my ear,
draw stories from perfect
rooted insinuations.

Countries into Words

So many languages, so many
I no longer can discern....

They become beautiful nonsense:

a tangled necklace of sound.

Yesterday I stood on the back
of a *songthaew*, holding on as it drove
the island road into town.
Disembarking, I
walked the beach
looking for a friend,
finding nothing, but
anonymity.

Laem Sai

Twilight breeze
like the slow
long seductive
first line
that lures you

all the way out to that cape: scorched rock
where one beach spills into
the next—sandy Maenam,
fugitive river that evaporates
before foreign eyes.

The rocks—sun blisters or chameleons?—
singed now, tattooed with dusk.

In a mess of foliage a shadow
                            or a shoulder
flits, darts through tall bushes.
The hour refuses
to be seen.

Behind me the cicadas suddenly
sing electric,
increasingly potent
decibels of another world.

I have nothing to fear
from fallen angels and sirens.
The lack of their noise is not silence.

A Better Heaven

Clouds the shape of arrows,
the colour of peaches,
of gold dust and chilies.

The dream-island in the gulf
is a statue to mountains.

Rumours of Thai boxing, of water
buffalo fights in days
without purpose.

      *   *   *

I feel the absence of
neighbours who have left.

The water is sad with seaweed, sodden.
Men try to sell hammocks,
open discreet boxes of gems,
                    "from Burma"
he said as if that country is
a better heaven.

Haad Rin

1

Already the morning
is fevered and swollen

as full as the first boat to Koh Phangan,
the island on the wistful
horizon except on hazy days.

We transfer to a boat long-tailed
like a ring-necked pheasant.

2

        Water-taxi to Baan Khaay,
a furious sun, the dusty road
by motorbike to Thongsala.
Humble night without shower
or reading light,
only a mosquito net,
a sheet full of sand.
I wake several times
to the crow
that scrapes
at dawn's dark soot.

3

Sleeping again on the morning boat
back to Samui, disembarking,
returning to places
intimately foreign, yet nostalgic
for the lifetime I missed overnight.
The day is overcast: Koh Phangan
has disappeared again
like a promise gone,
a promise disrespectfully unkept
when I could have
saved the day.

Coming inland

You can't know the mind-drifts,
the dreams between sentences.

But when can I come inland?

When I say dream
I mean meditation in a hot season
                    of salt spray and wind.

Josh says fishing means patience.
His renovated Chinese junk from Singapore,
his quiet brown Sri Lankan smile.
You can come inland anywhere, he says.

Or you can go out to bays,
private white beaches,
anchor down through
clear water to coral
meandering between delta and inlet,
water and land.

Anchored off Koh Tao

Snorkeling in the afternoon
                    —shaft of sunlight
        through the water like a plank,
        the soft crunch of fish
        eating coral.

Evening of hauling up small anchors
of squid hooked
to how we move away from
the rhythms of yesterday
when we were all eyes for the islands.

Clouds along the horizon—no sunset.
We spread dinner on the top deck:
barbecued garoupa, other catches.
A kerosene lamp in the middle
makes light a liqueur.

Then the orchestra of cicadas
the lift
of their arms
conducts graphed arches of sound

that fall as they
drown the dusk
with their pulse.

I'm here forever

The moon at the end of this Thai village
was full last night,
is full again tonight
somewhere else.
No one knows
where I am
since miniature white horses
race left to right on the water line.
Tropical storm winds, satay,
the perpetual bottle of water.
We get on
              like a thatch roofed bungalow
                        given a light,
like a mouth on fire
having tasted hot coconut milk curries
in these small worlds
where so many conjugations
of the present
are unfolding,
continuing
forever.

2533 in the Buddhist era

Between paragraphs of water,
of beaches, palm trees,
pages of conversation:
when you're this far ahead
there's no need to hurry.

Elephant heads
on the gate to the temple,
dogs sleeping in the sun,
monks saunter away in saffron robes,
the colour of the world's impermanence.

In search of Sandra

I go up river
in search of Sandra,
by water taxi,
up the Chao Phraya
in the city of Siamese angels.

Bangkok's river in May
is clouded brown,
the sky humid
and confused.

Near her guest house
I walk back lanes
where sun struggles
to light rain.
Wet leaves of fuchsia tease
high temple walls.

Sandra hasn't arrived,
her plans may have changed.
I write her a note
and leave.

Today I go up river again,
wait in the shadows
for the boat, watch a Thai boy
arrange on a platter
monk's flower
for Buddha
and vegetables for sale.

Then I go down river

revising my plans.

Some things about Thailand
I forgot to tell you

1
We ate python,
cobra and crocodile steak
at the Kaithong restaurant, Chiang Mai
served with a rich onion gravy.
It's not true that I'll eat anything.

2
The five-year old Thai boys selling roses
in the pub are as frail as their flowers.

And just as sharp.

3
My favourite temple in Sukhothai's
old city has
a tall shadowy Buddha
obscured behind two pillars:
its tentative
disclosure of heroic
               long fingers,
                   bronze fingernails
when all the other temples
are ruins of crumbled red brick.
Give me your hand so I'll be further astonished.

4
Sky is my last guest house in Thailand,
the sky a road the sun takes
to get to
this flat place.

No time for
the Dream Café
before leaving town.

INDIA

They were moments of affecting human joy and gentleness, when the decay of a city seemed as irrelevant as the splendid indifference of the now invisible mountain walls.

...we saw one of the images of the goddess [Saraswati, the goddess of learning and music]...clad in a purple robe with gold stars and holding a sitar made of gilded cardboard and tinsel; she was awaiting the procession in two days' time when she would be taken out with great music and chanting and in a final ceremony be dipped into a sacred tank whose waters would disssolve her body of unbaked clay.

— George Woodcock

Humayun's Tomb

I sit in the dry sandstone shade
of Delhi, on the roof of Humayun's tomb.
My frayed map, my being here, the dry trees

and the white mosque,
Dum Duma Sahib Gurudwara,
its windows boarded up
like a book
we close
when life at random breaks in.

Humayun's tomb
                -in-a-garden,
forerunner of the Taj Mahal.

Humayun's tomb in a dry garden
where the trees thirst
one leaf at a time
for the rains.

At the National Museum

We look at statues of Hindu gods
—Vishnu, Shiva, Brahma,
and goddesses whose breasts are full

from a divine era
when men unwrapped
and suckled saried women in the streets.

We wander through statued corridors,
cool passageways textured in marble,
collect other travellers, talk
of everything.

Later, shops full of multi-coloured
papier-mâché boxes, of soft gauze
gold-trimmed fabric.
                        I ask a woman
about her
forehead's red jewel.

I wear my sari tonight
like a beautiful challenge
all the way home
to the air-conditioned Hotel Rajdoot
on Mathura Road.

Thirteen Hours

We're almost late for the train in old Delhi
because our rickshaw driver
searched the streets
for the big rupee.

Our running foolish—
nothing punctual in this country
of colonial dust and monsoon.

The bus in Chandrigarh
was late too.
Now I sleep away flat land, farmland,
wake as the bus climbs steep hills.
Still far to go too slowly,
too quickly around sharp mountain turns
when I wish for the river below.
We stop for meals
and ponderous snacks, the too public toilet.

My eyes bear the weight
of India's hard questions.

      * * *

It takes forever to get
to this moment
after a musty dark sleep:

doors opening

to unrestrained snow on the mountains.

At the Turquoise Pension

This is not the coconut isle Samui
where the coconuts fall with a fury
and the palm leaves quiver the wind,
where the April festival of water
is thrown at you in soft silver bowls.

This is not crazy Delhi with its dust
and white cows. Not the Rajdoot hotel
with its mouldy wool, mothballs
in the bathroom drains.

This is not rickshaw drivers around
Connaught Circus upping the rate
by tens of rupees and men selling and selling
and children wanting.

This is Manali in the morning,
tea under an apple tree
in the northern state of Himachal Pradesh.
Birds sing in the green fruit trees
beckoning a pedlar who climbs
up past goat herds and sheep.

Into the mornings of the turquoise pension
comes the pedlar with his pack,
its bright coloured patches
and mirrors and tassels.
He wanders, calling

saffron   musk   saffron?

The Cobra of Palwal

Inside my terracotta vase, coil of dry rope,
I rise to the slow unsteady notes of a flute,
shimmy up a thread
of smoke, pulsate
to the last dream before
the promised breakfast, the dream
of a she-snake letting down her hood.
I rise to that melody of charm,
for the buses that come from the north
bring better meals.
Then they leave, heading for the Taj.

I would never dance there,
in that marble,
and gems like flowers of amber.
I would not frolic, fetter away
my sleep on such paleness,
tucked inside
that royal indulgence.

Why don't you take a walk,
down to the Jamuna, that old river,
and wade all the way in?

A reply

Lapis lazuli, bracelets of moonstone—
that man in the shop of jewels
desperate to sell anything.

Now birds fly slowly away
from the wide and shallow Jamuna,
its name like a woman's.
A man stands beside the river
screaming that the world will end.
Why is he *here*
by these gentle waters
and a palace of love?

TURKEY

It is well-known that Turks, that is to say the rude mass of the nation, regard all the mentally deranged as inspired by a divine spirit.

— Hans Christian Andersen
in Constantinople, 1841

Anthology of tiles

To talk in tiles,
the effervescent blues and greens
in the palace Topkapi,
talk as old as Byzantium,
roses of Constantinople.

To talk in tiles
scarved in history,
anthologies of colour and praise,
exquisite poetry, slender dancing,
16th century blue tulips,
stylized roses, leaves curled
like peonies on the underglazed panel
of the sultan's tomb.

If only I could talk
in Turkish tiles,
pattern my thoughts as beautifully
and rhyme with the walls
in the Room of Holy Relics
          —hair from the beard of Muhammad,
                          Muhammad's tooth—
and these eloquent blooms.

June 5, 1990
Istanbul, Turkey

Sound & Light Show at the Blue Mosque

the sound & light show in which voices personifying Istanbul
& the Blue Mosque bellow out verse over a Hollywood
soundtrack is (needless to say) as tacky as Warhol
                                    Let's Go Europe 1990

Like the blue profusion of flowers on tiles
the voice of Istanbul
is soft and rich.
It is female, lighting up
the nights in four languages.

Three evenings of proud incomprehensible
mysteries, exclamations of sound
as we sit on benches
outside the theatre of the Blue Mosque.

In the royal blue air
darkening with doubts and rivalry
the light searches, captures
domes, niches, terraces, the six minarets.

But the fourth night—Istanbul, she speaks
in my language,
speaks softly, woefully of history,
invasion and conquests.

Then the male voice of the architect
hesitant, fearful of the sultan.

Outdo Aya Sofya is the command.
Outdo, outshine.

In this theatre we witness
the architect's sculpted relief.

A Day in the Life

I have gazed at the beauty of Aya Sofya
with prayers round and brilliant blue
written in graceful swirls and loops and long curls.
I have stood many nights outside the Blue Mosque,
walked through the Gate
of the White Eunuchs at Topkapi;
found foxgloves and roses, the terrace
view of the Golden Horn
and Bosphorus; contemplated Iznik tiles,
old calligraphies, carpets too numerous to mention.
I have drunk *raki* with a sweet-talking Cypriot.
Beware! Men who purr loudly
will later roar. I have crossed a bridge,
have seen the city
from atop Galata Tower.

From there the city is so peaceful
and as overcast
as lion's milk and water.

On the beach at Hanedam

The milky heat of a white
sheeted hotel room in Izmir.

The vivid sharp lines of white buildings
in the dry air.

The scraggy hills smelling
of musty cranberries and bramble.

The trees that could bear olives
in a holy land.

The men named Mohammed, Hassan,
and Ali Baba.

The water's apparent clarity
in coves of undiscovered depths.

The smooth pebbles that brush
off a wet arm and dry in a fine seabreeze.

The creamy white stones
that make the fairest tanned.

The days a cloudless,
pale blue sky. The long lovely evenings.

The silvery-gold water humming
to the rocks, the fishermen of old Foça.

All of this
three days on the Aegean
where the weariness of travelling alone
and the talking only to my journal
is completely, utterly
dispelled. Dark words
after the long journey,
dark words bleached
with sun and salt,
so that, now, the many words
of my being here   shine.

Ater a car collided with the Izmir bus

We dine alone in the kitchen
on yogurt, stuffed peppers, Turkish salad;
help ourselves to sour wine

and talk of his near death in Romania,
a child with a ruptured appendix
in a hospital hallway,
ostracized and scorned
for being a Jew.

The kitchen darkening the wine.

      *   *   *

Now there is only a table
and words....
              What do you mean "dreamy"? I ask.

He who turned to look at me
when I touched a rain-damp bough,
when I picked tree bark off the sand,

he who leaves me wondering
about the archaeology
of anger.

City of Legend

The statue of Diana
looking as if she could nurse
whole nations, busts of Plato.
Socrates looking like the lion
in the Wizard of Oz.

In everything of greatness there is some illusion.

The Virgin Mary came here,
after the death of Christ. The drive
to her house and tomb, on the mountain.

We pass peach orchards,
fields that glow a dry gold
in the late afternoon.

Further up the long winding road
we enter a grove of trees.

In everything of greatness there is some illusion.

The leaves are biblical.

Goats graze by the roadside.
In a small house a woman kneels,
absorbed in prayer. I understand
why Mary wanted to come to this place,
to live out her days far from the stories,
the wagging tongues

like those of the silversmiths
who drove St. Paul from the city
for fear people would buy
his words and not their shrines.

In Ephesus we walk the many steps
of the Great Theatre, look down
at the stones around the stage.
Do the hills still conceal some treasure?
The Library of Celus squeezed
between two buildings, its upper columns
appear as thick as the ones below.
Illusion from the Latin, *to play*.

Just beyond my balcony,
creamy red roses.
Sharp winged swallows dive.
Across the street a sheep in a weedy lot.

I read that Mary Magdalene
is also buried here,
in this city
of significant women.

Aegean Magic

1

I've been given two beautiful peaches,
the most erotic of fruit.
A guest house breakfast in the country
of the temple of Artemis.

As I make a list
of the new wonders of the world,
new countries of contentment.

2

At a restaurant
glasses of red wine
like discreet flowers
appear out of nowhere.

I write of love
and public foreplay,
how his hand was a shape
containing pulses.

If only every poem
began or insinuated
our kissing in the back street
at the bottom of the stairs.

3

A tree with pale pale leaves.
Turn your head and the water is
turquoise, a gelatin
that hasn't quite set.

So why do we consider magic
to be only black
or white?

GREECE

I think how simple life is, just like this cell; what an innocent and sacred contact love is, just like the water the thirsty drink, bare without any sentimentality.

— Nikos Kazantzakis

Greek Salad Days

Stars painted silver
on cobalt blue ceiling domes,
the silhouette of churches, complete towns
of white on white on blue
—landscape for a watercolourist.

Olives as dark as deep space,
tzatziki, thick Greek yogurt and honey
and more salad: the ingredients
of new wonders.

This world that lives by turquoise.

I sit in cafés all day
saturated and replete,
writing of the taste of salt,

of this satiable earth.

Women of Questions

Two women under lemon trees in a courtyard
wringing out hand-washing
to hang on the line.

Breakfast of coffee, yogurt and honey,
"You don't have to answer these questions"
I say, as she talks of miscarriages,
how she gave up trying
before the marriage failed,
her mother dying of pneumonia last year.

Her eyes remember.
Tears, the soul at low tide.

I lean over, touch her knee—
sympathy a path we take
too carefully.

"No," she pauses, "no, I want to." This helps
as, reaching for fullness,
she talks the tide in
asks about travelling alone,
paying tribute with a simple question.
"And you?"

She will walk through Samos town
and I will write.

I will write.

The Muse in Samos town

The back streets are cobbled and narrow.
The sweet night air smells of jasmine.
I imagine someone walking up to me,
handing me a small bottle, delicate,
the colour of lilacs, with a glass stopper
that slips so easily
into the neck of the flask.

        "Here" he says,
"here is the perfumed night air
of Samos town."
And he leaves.

This gift may not settle the questions
about the Temple of Hera,
its many columns not yet unearthed,
won't make the Greek islands more
to tourists' liking than Turkey,
won't stop the Greek woman
at the pension from throwing up her hands
before she goes off to change the sheets.

But try it—breathe in
the scent of something you love,
of a particular place, lose yourself
in narrow cobbled streets.

Kokkari Postcard

A white table surrounded
by four fraying canvas chairs;
on it glasses of ice water,
a bouquet of bougainvillea,
a small pink vase
and four empty bowls of ice cream.

Behind the table tall waves
splash white froth
on the seawall,

                    sea-acres
of turquoise and royal blue beyond.

You do not see
the car that brought me here,
the children
who ate the ice cream,
who played with the cocktail parasols,
the Greek waitress
taking away
the cups and bowls and glasses.

June 25, 1990
Kokkari, Samos, Greece

Pulling the tide

This land, the guidebook says,
is the land of Amazons.

Am I at home here?

In this land
I can bare myself,
my breasts and long legs
on a rocky beach,
my arms pulling the tide toward me.

After 4 p.m., Psili Ammos beach

What colour is this sudden solitude
when the water is turquoise
lapping at my quiet door?

When wind might break
the dry bush beside me?

When the rocks slope at angles
to the island?

This solitude—
is it a different colour
than yesterday's port town?
The drone of a motorbike
travelling towards it?

Solitude's colour
is the colour I turn as I arouse myself
sunbathing naked on a private beach,
dazzling myself to a gloss.

SPAIN

Blessings on him who invented sleep, the mantle that covers all human thoughts, the food that appeases hunger, the drink that quenches thirst, the fire that warms cold, the cold that moderates heat, and, lastly, the general coin that purchases all things, the balance and weight that equals the shepherd with the king, and the simple with the wise.

— Miquel de Cervantes

No Photos of Costa del Sol

The tissue paper sky wrinkles.
What is this, *picturesque?*

We are not innocent

of acts of omission
or exclusion. I lie topless in the sun
feeling the slightest wind
around my breasts.

Guilty of pictures,
we are too innocent
of all the senses.

Throw away your camera
and the pictures framed in quarantine.
You could be
fulfilled, without any pictures
of Spain's day of Independence—a day
which can also be ours.

October 12, 1990
Benalmádena, Costa del Sol

Some Aspects of the Reales Alcázares

The polychrome walls look crochetted.
Bamboo could be green marble.
A duck shivers alone
in one corner of a pond,
presumably dying.
There are magnolia trees,
trees with pink blossoms,
flowers like white trumpets,
leaves of sienna leather,
tiles on the walls like a children's game,
some mismatched and faded.
The reigning colours: salmon pink, terracotta,
sunburnt gold, and white.
The flowers and blossoms
unrecognizably exotic
to even the horticulturist
with whom I strolled.
We got lost in the garden
but found coats of arms, balconies,
royal carriages, and fountains,
Renaissance ceilings
and tiled courtyards
that were once gardens
and gardens
and yet another garden in the walls.

The Glory of the Doves

After drawings of the new world
at Archives of the Indies,
the sun comes out,
the rio Guadalquiver green
with shadows of tree silk.

How my sense of well-being grows
like a date palm
earthquaked out of saffron-gold earth,
its fruits the most fragile
of Christmas ornaments.

Then this magic Christmas palm
changes—never static
never so thin—
to one white dove,
wings the colour of yogurt.

But then I come into a plaza
where school children lunch
around hedges and benches,
eat ice cream and feed the birds
in this plaza called
"The Glory of the Doves,"
these birds at my feet who were
everywhere I walked.

And this was more beautiful
than coincidence.

Oct. 17, 1990
Sevilla, Spain

Sevilla Cathedral

Ceramic frogs sit in the park
and birds sing around fountains
although there is litter and flies.

The remains of Columbus are here
at the entrance of the church
"so great that those
who will come after us
will take us for madmen."

The vaulted ceilings, cobwebbed stone
fishnetted above paintings and pillars.

Woodcarvings, alcoves honouring saints
and later rooms I almost overlook: full
of silver, costumes, embroidered
robes and headpieces.

And then I climb to the top
of Giraldi Tower, look down.
The city whitewashed, gold trimmed.
The orange trees,
static green moons
from the time of the Moors.

But up here: the pillars and arches,
the palm trees of rooftop terraces,
the trellis, the ivy,
the fireworks on this roof
all such tender stone.

TRANSLATIONS

...become a pilgrim who visits the clouds
       and pays his respects to the rocks.
The waters have a secret method
       for flowing beyond this world;
the mountains are like a drug
       for lightening the body.
Before the eyes, Mount Hua—
       a wall of 10, 000 feet.
On the robe—a single speck of dust from the city.
If you come across a chessboard, stay for a while:
before you know it, the wildflowers
       will fade
       and bloom again.

— Yuan Hung-tao

The same weight as water

I have lost home and gained the world:
a marriage. I learn: that travellers share

that I can be rude when necessary
that I can sleep anywhere

that I love the potential of the road
that my address book is too small

that I can arrive in cities at midnight
that I would beg if I had to

that I carry the pack on my back
on a road that walks with me

that rivers run through my heart
as do all the waters of the world

that nobody is only their country
so how will we translate ourselves?

that the world is small
with mutual friends

that I've met only one percent
of everyone I want to know

that images of such energetic beauty
and ugliness keep running

beyond themselves
that it doesn't matter who we are

that I become whatever I travel to,
become the same weight as water.

Acknowledgements

I want to thank the editors of the following periodicals where some of these poems first appeared: *Acta Victoriana, The Antigonish Review, Arc, Canadian Literature, Contemporary Verse 2, The Dalhousie Review, Dandelion, The Gaspereau Review, Grain, Kairos, The Last Word Anthology, McGill Street, The Nashwaak Review, The New Quarterly, paperplates, Pottersfield Portfolio, Prairie Journal, Queen's Quarterly, Room of One's Own, TickleAce, The White Wall Review* and *The Windsor Review*.

Much gratitude to the Banff Centre for the Arts, to Robert Hilles, Don McKay, Jan Zwicky, and Rachel Wyatt.

I especially want to thank the members of the Halifax Poetry Group for their support, encouragement, camaraderie, and dedication to all our words.

I also want to thank Eleanore Schönmaier, for the photographs; Donna and Michael Sharpe for providing a home away from home; and Sue MacLeod, Bruce Hunter, and Alistair MacLeod for their readings of the manuscript. *Tapadh leibh!*

Finally, I'd like to express my heartfelt thanks and gratitude to Joy Gugeler and to all those fellow travellers who lightened the load.